Cowgirls & Cocktails

First published in Great Britain in 2026 by
Michael O'Mara Books Limited
9 Lion Yard
Tremadoc Road
London SW4 7NQ

EU representative:
Authorised Rep Compliance Ltd
Ground Floor, 71 Baggot Street Lower
Dublin D02 P593
Ireland

Copyright © Michael O'Mara Books Limited 2026

All rights reserved. You may not copy, store, distribute, transmit, reproduce or otherwise make available this publication (or any part of it) in any form, or by any means (electronic, digital, optical, mechanical, photocopying, recording, machine readable, text/data mining or otherwise), without the prior written permission of the publisher. Any person who does any unauthorized act in relation to this publication may be liable to criminal prosecution and civil claims for damages.

A CIP catalogue record for this book is available from the British Library.

This product is made of material from well-managed, FSC®-certified forests and other controlled sources. The manufacturing processes conform to the environmental regulations of the country of origin.

For further information see www.mombooks.com/about/sustainability-climate-focus
Report any safety issues to product.safety@mombooks.com and see
www.mombooks.com/contact/product-safety

UK edition:
ISBN: 978-1-78929-898-7 in hardback print format

US edition:
ISBN: 978-1-78929-899-4 in hardback print format

1 2 3 4 5 6 7 8 9 10

Recipe developer: Denise Smart
Contributor: Liz Marvin
Cover design by Jade Wheaton
Designed, illustrated and typeset by Jade Wheaton
Printed and bound in China by WKT
www.mombooks.com

Cowgirls & Cocktails

60 COUNTRY MUSIC INSPIRED COCKTAILS FOR SIPPIN' PRETTY

Michael O'Mara Books Limited

Contents

Something in the Orange Spritz 6
Tequila Never Broke My Heart 8
I Walk the Lime 10
Cowboy Carter-ita 12
Save a Horse (Rye'd a Cowboy) 14
Man! I Feel Like a Woo Woo 16
Slim Pickle 18
6 Mules Later 20
Fast Sidecar 22
The Giver Gimlet 24
No Shoes, No Shirt, Negroni 26
Four Score He Cheats 28
Aust-Gin Aviation 30
Follow Your Amaretto 32
Stand by Your Manhattan 34
Whiskey on My Mind 36
Jolene's Revenge 38
Boot Scootin' Spritz 40
Shaboozy Sling 42
Red Solo Royale 44
Neon Moon Martini 46
Teardrops on My Bar Cart 48
I Will Always Love Yuzu 50
Friends in Lowball Glasses 52
Strawberry Wine Cooler 54
Long Islands in the Stream 56
Achy Breaky Bloody Mary 58
Honky Tonk Hurricane 60
Wildflowers and Whiskey 62

9 to 5 O'Clock Somewhere **64**
Ring of Fireball **66**
Drinkin' 'Bout Me **68**
Something in the Watermelon Daquiri **70**
Spicy Margaritaville **72**
I'm Not Americano's Sweetheart **74**
If It Weren't for the Wine **76**
Tennessee Whiskey Sour **78**
Blue Curaçao Ain't Your Color **80**
Wagon Wheel Wrecker **82**
Fancy Like Fizz **84**
Highball Horse **86**
Son of a Sinnerman **88**
Take Me Home, Cosmo Roads **90**
Texas Hold My Cocktail **92**
When It Rains It Pours Whiskey **94**
Need Brew Now **96**
Gin McGraw **98**
(I Never Promised You a) Rosé Garden **100**
Mai Tai Church **102**
Hazy **104**
Paloma Smokeshow **106**
Limoncello Like You Mean It **108**
Goodbye Earl Grey Sour **110**
Sweet Vermouth Alabama **112**
Drinkin' After Midnight **114**
Sloe Burn **116**
French 23 **118**
Buy Dirty Martini **120**
Mean Mojito **122**
Long Long Tom Collins **124**
Index **126**

Something in the Orange Spritz

There's something quietly magical about a slow sunset and a spritz in hand. Just like Zach Bryan's haunting anthem, this bittersweet cocktail captures the ache of something left unsaid. With its bold hue, gentle bubbles and a poetic hint of orange blossom, this spritz is perfect for sipping at golden hour, when the sky's on fire and the night hasn't quite begun.

Ingredients

Serves: 1

- ice cubes, for the glass
- 60 ml (2 oz) Aperol
- 90 ml (3 oz) prosecco, chilled
- 2 drops of orange blossom water (optional)
- 30 ml (2 tbsp) blood orange soda water, or to taste
- 1 dehydrated orange wheel, to garnish

Method

1. Fill a large wine glass with ice.
2. Add the Aperol followed by the prosecco and the orange blossom water, if using. Top up with soda water and stir gently to combine.
3. Garnish with an orange wheel to serve.

SOUNDTRACK: 'Something in the Orange' by Zach Bryan

Tequila Never
Broke My Heart

Whether, like Luke Combs, your truck has broken down and you've had a disappointing fishing trip, or it's more of a case of a bad day at work and terrible traffic, we all need something we can rely on not to let us down at the end of a day. So why not get on the group chat with this sweet cocktail in hand and share some jokes and memes with those you can count on?

Ingredients

Serves: 1

15 ml (1 tbsp) grenadine

60 ml (2 oz) silver tequila

125 ml (4 oz) mango or mango and orange juice

30 ml (2 tbsp) freshly squeezed lime juice

ice cubes, for the shaker and the glass

1 cocktail cherry and an orange or lime wheel, to garnish

Method

1. Pour the grenadine into the bottom of a hurricane glass.

2. Place the tequila, mango and lime juices into a cocktail shaker with a handful of ice and shake until the shaker is cold.

3. Add some ice to the glass and strain the contents of the shaker carefully over the grenadine and ice, to create vivid layers like a sunset.

4. Garnish the glass with a cocktail cherry and a citrus wheel before serving.

SOUNDTRACK: 'Beer Never Broke My Heart' by Luke Combs

I Walk the Lime

The ultimate tribute to the 'man in black' himself, this is based on the 'rickey' cocktail, invented in the 1880s in Washington DC, in Shoomaker's Bar on Pennsylvania Avenue. You can make it with gin or vodka, too, but this version uses gin to keep it well south of the Mason-Dixon line, as befits a country music great who was born in Arkansas and became one of the best-loved adopted sons of Nashville, Tennessee.

Ingredients

Serves: 1

ice cubes, for the glass
45 ml (1½ oz) gin
freshly squeezed juice of ½ lime
125–175 ml (4–6 oz) soda water

2–3 lime wheels, to garnish

Method

1. Fill a tall glass with ice cubes.
2. Pour over the gin and add the lime juice, then give it a good stir. Pour over the soda water and stir gently.
3. Drop in the lime wheels and enjoy.

SOUNDTRACK: 'I Walk the Line' by Johnny Cash

Cowboy Carter-ita

A cocktail with beer and chillies in it? It may sound crazy as all get out, but don't knock it till you try it. Queen Bey sticks to nobody's rules – and neither should you. Like halftime at the Super Bowl, this drink puts on quite a show. It has a salty, spicy kick that comes out of nowhere and is guaranteed to rock your world.

Ingredients

Serves: 1

6 thin slices of fresh green jalapeños
ice cubes, for the shaker
50 ml (1¾ oz) tequila
30 ml (2 tbsp) freshly squeezed lime juice
30 ml (2 tbsp) triple sec
50 ml (1¾ oz) Mexican lager, chilled

1 orange and 1 lime wheel, to garnish

For the salt rim
2 tsp coarse sea salt
1 lime wedge

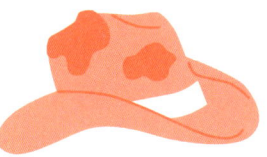

Method

1. First, prepare the glass. Place the salt on a small plate, run the lime wedge along the rim of a martini glass, then dip the rim of the glass into the salt. Stand the glass upright and leave to dry.

2. Place 3 of the jalapeño slices into the bottom of a cocktail shaker and muddle. Add the ice and all the liquid ingredients apart from the lager. Shake vigorously for 20–30 seconds until well chilled.

3. Strain the drink into the prepared martini glass and top with the lager. Garnish with the orange and lime wheels and remaining jalapeño slices and serve immediately.

SOUNDTRACK: *Cowboy Carter* by Beyoncé

Save a Horse
(Rye'd a Cowboy)

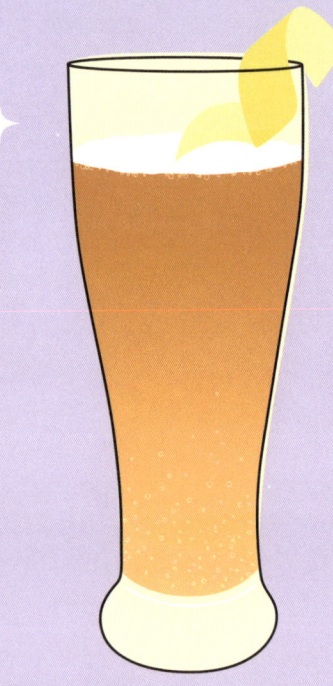

Beer and whiskey in the same glass? Hell, why not?! Keep it real Southern-style with this tasty tribute to a fun and irreverent country party song. Maybe it sounds a bit much, not like something you'd be into, maybe you're even rolling your eyes. But hey, it could be that channelling some country bro energy and making some noise with a beer cocktail in hand is exactly what you need.

Ingredients

Serves: 1

60 ml (2 oz) whiskey

30 ml (2 tbsp) freshly squeezed lemon juice

15 ml (1 tbsp) Simple Syrup (see below)

ice cubes, for the shaker

200 ml (7 oz) lager, chilled

1 piece of lemon peel, to garnish

For the Simple Syrup

300g (10 oz) caster (baker's) sugar

150ml (¼ pt) water

1 sterilized jar, for storage

Method

1. To make the syrup, place the sugar and water in a pan and heat gently over a low-medium heat, stirring until the sugar has dissolved.

2. Bring to the boil, then take off the heat and let it cool. Store in a jar in the fridge for up to 1 month.

3. Place the whiskey, lemon juice and simple syrup into a cocktail shaker with a handful of ice. Shake until the shaker is really cold.

4. Strain into a 300 ml (½ pt) beer glass and top with the lager. Stir to mix and garnish with the lemon twist.

SOUNDTRACK: 'Save a Horse (Ride a Cowboy)' by Big & Rich

Man! I Feel Like a Woo Woo

Shania Twain's timeless hit sounds exactly like pop and country met in a bar and turned the night into the best party imaginable. Just like the song that inspired it, this fun and carefree cocktail is all about letting your hair down and going where the night takes you. Who needs a date when you can shake up some cocktails and sing and dance with your besties?

Ingredients

Serves: 1

50 ml (1¾ oz) vodka
25 ml (¾ oz) peach schnapps
75 ml (3 oz) cranberry juice, chilled
15 ml (1 tbsp) freshly squeezed lime juice
ice cubes, for the shaker and the glass

1 lime wheel, to garnish

Method

1. Place the vodka, schnapps, cranberry and lime juice into a cocktail shaker with a large handful of ice. Shake well until the shaker is very cold.

2. Add some ice to a tumbler or highball glass. Strain over the cocktail.

3. Garnish with a lime wheel.

SOUNDTRACK: 'Man! I Feel Like a Woman!' by Shania Twain

Slim Pickle

They say you've got to kiss a lot of frogs to find your prince or princess, but there are times when it seems like there are just frogs everywhere. So, if your love life is suffering from a serious drought, gather your gang together and whip up this fittingly slightly sour drink. Just like Sabrina tells us in this anthem to a lack of romantic options, sometimes you just need to have a good ol' moan.

Ingredients

Serves: 1

30 ml (2 tbsp) gin
25 ml (1 oz) sweet and sour apple liqueur
15 ml (1 tbsp) pickle juice
15 ml (1 tbsp) freshly squeezed lemon juice
15 ml (1 tbsp) freshly squeezed lime juice
ice cubes, for the shaker

1 cocktail gherkin and a thin slice of apple, to garnish

Method

1. Place all the ingredients, except the garnish but including the ice, into a cocktail shaker. Shake vigorously for about 20 seconds or until the shaker is very cold.

2. Strain into a chilled martini or coupe glass. Thread the cocktail gherkin onto a cocktail stick and use to garnish the glass along with the apple slice.

SOUNDTRACK: 'Slim Pickins' by Sabrina Carpenter

6 Mules Later

There's always that one person who, months after they let you down and broke your heart, gets in touch to say they made a mistake. But as Megan Moroney tells us in her anthem to coming back stronger after a break-up, you can't let yourself fall for the same old crap again. The ginger beer in this cocktail is like the fire in your belly that helps you to tell them to get right back under the rock they crawled out from.

Ingredients

Serves: 1

- ice cubes, for the tumbler and the shaker
- 50 ml (1¾ oz) vodka
- 15 ml (1 tbsp) freshly squeezed lime juice
- 125 ml (4 oz) fiery ginger beer
- 2 dashes of Angostura bitters
- 1 sprig of fresh mint and a lime wedge, to garnish

Method

1. Fill a copper mug or tumbler with ice cubes.
2. Place the vodka, lime juice and ginger beer into a cocktail shaker with a little ice and stir well.
3. Strain into the mug or tumbler and add the bitters. Garnish with a sprig of mint and a lime wedge.

SOUNDTRACK: '6 Months Later' by Megan Moroney

Fast Sidecar

Who hasn't dreamed of getting into a fast car that will take us away from our humdrum routine and speed us off to a whole new life? Luke Combs' cover of Tracy Chapman's classic song is wistful, full of longing and a little intense, just like this boozy, orange-tinged cocktail. Sip moodily as you think of driving across the border and leaving your old life behind.

Ingredients

Serves: 1

50 ml (1¾ oz) cognac

25 ml (1 oz) orange liqueur

25 ml (1 oz) freshly squeezed lemon juice

ice cubes, for the shaker

1 piece of orange peel, to garnish

Method

1. Place the cognac, orange liqueur and lemon juice into a cocktail shaker with a handful of ice cubes.

2. Shake well, then strain into a coupe glass. Twist the piece of orange peel over the glass to release its oil, then drop it into the glass.

SOUNDTRACK: 'Fast Car' by Luke Combs

The Giver Gimlet

A gimlet is a simple drink that gets to the point - just like Chappell Roan's sexy barnstormer about how she can offer so much more than the truck-driving boys of her hometown. You could just use shop-bought lime cordial, but making your own syrup, as per the recipe on the next page, brings a level of zing that the generic stuff just can't touch. Plus, Chappell would surely approve of going the extra mile to make sure everyone is satisfied.

Ingredients

Serves: 1

60 ml (2 oz) gin

ice cubes, for the shaker

1 lime wheel, to garnish

For the lime syrup
1 lime

200 g (7 oz) caster (baker's) sugar

Method

1. To make the lime syrup, finely grate the zest from the lime into a saucepan, then add the sugar. Cut the lime in half and squeeze the juice from both halves into a measuring jug. Top up with cold water to make 100 ml (3½ oz) and add to the pan. Place the pan over a low heat and heat, stirring continuously, for 3–4 minutes until the sugar has dissolved – do not allow the mixture to boil. Strain into a heatproof jug and allow to cool.

2. Pour the gin, 50 ml (2 oz) of the lime syrup and a handful of ice cubes into a cocktail shaker. (Any leftover syrup can be stored in the fridge for up to 1 month.) Shake for about 20 seconds until the shaker is very cold.

3. Strain into a chilled coupe or martini glass and garnish with the lime wheel.

SOUNDTRACK: 'The Giver' by Chappell Roan

No Shoes, No Shirt
Negroni

The passion fruit liqueur that replaces the vermouth in this otherwise classic negroni is the sweet treat that means it's holiday time. It's the straw cowboy hat pulled low against the bright sunshine, the kicking off of your boots to feel the sand between your toes, the knowing that the blues are behind you and there's nothing to do but relax. It's not just a cocktail, it's the laidback life we all want to be living.

Ingredients

Serves: 1

25 ml (¾ oz) passion fruit liqueur

25 ml (¾ oz) gin

25 ml (¾ oz) Campari

2 large ice cubes, for the shaker and the glass

1 piece of orange peel, to garnish

Method

1. Add all the liquid ingredients to a cocktail shaker with a large handful of ice cubes and stir everything together.

2. Place the large ice cubes into an old fashioned glass and strain over the cocktail.

3. Garnish with the twist of orange peel.

SOUNDTRACK: 'No Shoes, No Shirt, No Problems' by Kenny Chesney

Four Score
He Cheats

While vandalizing someone's car is probably not a great idea, even if they are a lowdown dirty cheat, whipping up this absolute treat of a drink definitely is. You don't need to have a thirst for revenge for this grown-up, sophisticated cocktail to hit the spot. Fun fact: the 'four score' drink this is based on was invented by famous Savoy head barman Joe Gilmore for Winston Churchill's eightieth birthday – hence the name. You don't get more of a pedigree than that.

Ingredients

Serves: 1

45 ml (1½ oz) brandy
30 ml (2 tbsp) Lillet Blanc
15 ml (1 tbsp) Yellow Chartreuse
ice cubes, for the shaker

1 piece of lemon peel, to garnish

Method

1. Place all the liquid ingredients into a cocktail shaker, add a handful of ice cubes and stir well.

2. Strain into a coupe glass and garnish with a twist of lemon peel.

SOUNDTRACK: 'Before He Cheats' by Carrie Underwood

Aust-Gin
Aviation

Sometimes you gotta pack up, get out and leave the unreliable guy behind - he's never going to match your energy or your ambition. That's what Dasha does in this country banger, and here's a cocktail to celebrate moving on from someone who doesn't deserve you. This drink's unusual lilac hue, which comes from the crème de violette, is a reminder to stand out and forge your own path, rather than settling for the mundane.

Ingredients

Serves: 1

ice cubes, for the shaker

50 ml (1¾ oz) gin

15 ml (1 tbsp) freshly squeezed lemon juice

15 ml (1 tbsp) maraschino liqueur

15 ml (1 tbsp) crème de violette

1–2 maraschino cherries and a piece of lemon peel, to garnish

Method

1. Add the ice and all the other ingredients, apart from the garnish, to a cocktail shaker and shake for about 20 seconds, or until the shaker is very cold to the touch.

2. Strain into a martini glass. Thread the cherries onto a cocktail stick and use to garnish the drink with the lemon peel.

SOUNDTRACK: 'Austin (Boots Stop Workin')' by Dasha

Follow Your **Amaretto**

This unusual sour is the perfect accompaniment to Kacey Musgraves' anthem about ignoring the judgement of others and finding your own path. Almond liqueur, lemon and cherry juice might not be the most obvious combo, but sometimes you gotta shake things up ... Add a little more lemon juice if you like a sour kick, or a little more cherry juice to sweeten things up – the most important thing is that you do it your way.

Ingredients

Serves: 1

- 50 ml (1¾ oz) amaretto
- 30 ml (2 tbsp) freshly squeezed lemon juice
- 5 ml (1 tsp) syrup from a jar of maraschino cherries
- 15 ml (1 tbsp) egg white or aquafaba (chickpea water)
- ice cubes, for the shaker
- 1–3 maraschino cherries, to garnish

Method

1. Place the amaretto, lemon juice, cherry syrup and egg white into a cocktail shaker with a handful of ice cubes. Shake well, until the outside of the shaker is cold.

2. Strain the cocktail into a jug, discard the ice from the shaker and return the cocktail to the shaker along with the egg white and shake well so the egg white froths up.

3. Pour the cocktail into a chilled coupe or martini glass, thread the cherries onto a cocktail stick and use to garnish the glass.

SOUNDTRACK: 'Follow Your Arrow' by Kacey Musgraves

Stand by Your Manhattan

Classic, bold and unapologetically strong - just like Tammy herself - this cocktail is a tribute to loyalty, love and just a little bit of drama. The Stand By Your Manhattan sticks to tradition with whiskey, sweet vermouth and bitters, but adds a whisper of cherry liqueur for a sultry Southern kiss. Whether you're standing by your man, your girls or just your Friday night plans, this one's for slow dancing and telling it like it is.

Ingredients

Serves: 1

50 ml (1¾ oz) whiskey

25 ml (¾ oz) sweet vermouth

5 ml (1 tsp) cherry liqueur

2 dashes of Angostura bitters

ice cubes, for the glass

1 maraschino cherry or piece of orange peel, to garnish

Method

1. Add all the liquid ingredients to a mixing glass with the ice cubes. Stir until well chilled – about 20–30 seconds.

2. Strain into a chilled coupe or martini glass.

3. Garnish with a cherry, or an orange twist if you're feeling a little sharper.

SOUNDTRACK: 'Stand By Your Man' by Tammy Wynette

Whiskey on My Mind

There's no need to let the good times slip through your fingers, like the protagonist does in this soft, sad country classic by everyone's favourite outlaw, Willie Nelson, when you have bourbon and good company to hand. This smooth whiskey sipper goes down beautifully with the fruitiness of the peach and orange flavours. Just like how the gorgeous melody of the song both eases and amplifies the heartbreak.

Ingredients

Serves: 1

60 ml (2 oz) bourbon or other whiskey

30 ml (2 tbsp) freshly squeezed orange juice

15ml (1 tbsp) Ginger Syrup (see page 117)

30 ml (2 tbsp) peach schnapps

ice cubes, for the shaker, plus 1 large ice cube for the glass

1 peach slice, to garnish

Method

1. Pour the bourbon, orange juice, Ginger Syrup and peach schnapps into a cocktail shaker with a large handful of ice cubes. Shake until the cocktail shaker is really cold.

2. Place a large cube of ice into a lowball glass and strain over the cocktail. Garnish with the peach slice.

SOUNDTRACK: 'Always on My Mind' by Willie Nelson

Jolene's Revenge

Oh, Jolene . . . She had the smile, the hair, the gall to steal your man – but not any more. Inspired by Dolly Parton's iconic heartbreak anthem (and a healthy dose of revenge fantasy), this spicy, smoky cocktail brings the heat in all the right ways. With a bold kick of tequila, a flicker of chilli and just enough mezcal to smoulder, Jolene's Revenge is what you serve when you're done playing nice and are ready to dance with a little fire in your soul.

Ingredients

Serves: 1

2–3 slices of fresh red chilli
45 ml (1½ oz) tequila
15 ml (1 tbsp) mezcal
25 ml (¾ oz) freshly squeezed lime juice
20 ml (⅔ oz) agave syrup
dash of orange bitters
ice cubes, for the shaker and the glass

1 lime wheel and/or dried chilli, to garnish

Method

1. Rim the glass with lime juice and dip it in the chilli-salt blend. Set aside.
2. In a shaker, muddle the chilli slices (adjust for spice level).
3. Add the tequila, mezcal, lime juice, agave syrup and orange bitters.
4. Fill with ice and shake hard for about 15 seconds.
5. Strain into a tumbler glass over fresh ice (or one large cube).
6. Garnish with a lime wheel and/or a dried chilli for drama.

SOUNDTRACK: 'Jolene' by Dolly Parton

Boot Scootin' Spritz

Bubbly, playful and a little bit flirty, this is the perfect drink to sip as you're getting ready with your best friends for a night at the city limits honky tonk. The elderflower and mint go together like denim and denim, and the prosecco delivers that Fourth of July feeling - even if, in reality, it's a rainy day in November and the 'honky tonk' is your living room.

Ingredients

Serves: 1

½ lime, cut into 4 wheels

4 fresh mint leaves, plus a sprig to garnish

ice cubes, for the glass

30 ml (2 tbsp) gin

30 ml (2 tbsp) elderflower liqueur

100 ml (3¾ oz) prosecco, chilled

50 ml (1¾ oz) soda water, chilled, or to top

Method

1. Place half of the lime wheels and the mint leaves into the bottom of a large wine glass and muddle together.

2. Add some ice, then pour over the gin and elderflower liqueur and stir to mix. Add the prosecco, then top with the soda water.

3. Garnish with the remaining lime wheels and a sprig of mint.

SOUNDTRACK: 'Boot Scootin' Boogie' by Brooks & Dunn

Shaboozey Sling

The original sling style of cocktail was a simple drink made with a spirit, sugar and water. Just like the first country music bands were just a fiddle, a banjo and an acoustic guitar. But why limit yourself when there are so many more ingredients to play with? In this fun, long drink, the bitters bring the herbiness, while the ginger beer packs a punch and the sugar makes everything a little bit sweeter. So get your friends to the bar for a Shaboozey Sling - the more the merrier.

Ingredients

Serves: 1

- 60 ml (2 oz) whiskey
- 1 tsp caster (baker's) sugar
- 2 drops of Angostura bitters
- 30 ml (2 tbsp) freshly squeezed lime juice
- ice cubes, for the shaker and the glass
- ginger beer, chilled, to top
- 1 lime wheel, to garnish

Method

1. Add the whiskey, sugar, bitters and lime juice to a cocktail shaker along with a handful of ice and shake well until the shaker is cold.

2. Strain into a tall or highball glass, over ice. Top with the ginger beer and garnish with a lime wheel.

SOUNDTRACK: 'A Bar Song (Tipsy)' by Shaboozey

Red Solo Royale

Like the song, this drink is a tribute to keeping things real. Sure, sometimes you want to get out the fancy glasses and make a sophisticated, picture-perfect cocktail. But for a real American party you need red cups. Uniting bubbles and bourbon, this drink puts a down-home Southern twist on the classic royale – like sequins on denim or your best party dress worn with your comfiest boots.

Ingredients

Serves: 1

30 ml (2 tbsp) bourbon

30 ml (2 tbsp) black raspberry liqueur

15 ml (1 tbsp) freshly squeezed lemon juice

ice cubes, for the shaker and the glass

90 ml (3 oz) prosecco or champagne, chilled

1–2 fresh raspberries, to garnish

Method

1. Place the bourbon, black raspberry liqueur and lemon juice into a cocktail shaker with a handful of ice, then shake until the shaker is cold.

2. Fill a wine glass with ice, strain over the cocktail and top up with the prosecco or champagne.

3. Garnish with fresh raspberries.

SOUNDTRACK: 'Red Solo Cup' by Toby Keith

Neon Moon
Martini

With its vivid, unusual color, this is an eye-catching and unforgettable cocktail, just right to pay tribute to a song that's about sitting in the neon light cast from a bar sign, thinking about lost love and things that could never be. While it's not great to dwell too much on the past, a little moment of nostalgia and longing is all part of that complicated and beautiful experience that is being human.

Ingredients

Serves: 1

50 ml (1¾ oz) gin
30 ml (2 tbsp) crème de violette
15 ml (1 tbsp) blue curaçao
15 ml (1 tbsp) freshly squeezed lemon juice
ice cubes, for the shaker

1 piece of lemon peel, to garnish

Method

1. Place all the liquid ingredients into a cocktail shaker along with a large handful of ice and shake until the shaker is cold.

2. Strain into a martini glass and garnish with a twist of lemon peel.

SOUNDTRACK: 'Neon Moon' by Brooks & Dunn

Teardrops on My Bar Cart

This zesty, zingy cocktail is ready to tell it like it is, just like the Queen of Pop herself. Why do we fall in love with the wrong people? Why can't we just quit that one who doesn't see us the way we want them to? Who knows the solutions to these age-old problems, but poured into a sophisticated martini glass, this grown-up pink drink will at least look great in your hand as you contemplate the big questions of matters of the heart.

Ingredients

Serves: 1

45 ml (1½ oz) vodka or grapefruit vodka
60 ml (2 oz) freshly squeezed grapefruit juice
15ml (1 tbsp) freshly squeezed lemon juice
10 ml (2 tsp) triple sec
ice cubes, for the shaker

1 piece of grapefruit peel, to garnish

For the sugar rim

2 tsp caster (baker's) sugar
1 tsp finely grated grapefruit zest
1 small wedge of grapefruit

Method

1. For the sugar rim, mix together the sugar and grapefruit zest on a small plate. Rub the rim of a martini glass with the grapefruit wedge, then dip the rim into the sugar mix to coat. Stand upright and leave to dry.

2. Place all the liquid ingredients into a cocktail shaker along with a handful of ice and shake until the shaker is really cold.

3. Strain into the prepared glass and garnish with the grapefruit peel.

SOUNDTRACK: 'Teardrops On My Guitar' by Taylor Swift

I Will Always Love Yuzu

Often seen as a romantic love song, maybe thanks to Whitney Houston's version in the film *The Bodyguard*, Dolly actually wrote 'I Will Always Love You' for a friend. It's about knowing it's time to move on but always carrying your memories of the person you are leaving behind with you. The yuzu speaks to the bittersweet feelings in the song, and the ginger is the fire in your belly that keeps you moving forward, even when it's hard.

Ingredients

Serves: 1

ice cubes, for the glass

30 ml (2 tbsp) shochu or sake

45 ml (1½ oz) yuzu juice, or to taste

ginger beer, chilled, to top

1 lime wedge, to garnish

Method

1. Fill a lowball glass with ice, add the shochu or sake and yuzu juice. Top with the ginger beer and stir well.

2. Garnish with the lime wedge.

SOUNDTRACK: 'I Will Always Love You' by Dolly Parton

Friends in Lowball Glasses

This is the perfect late-night cocktail. It's smooth with a bluesy edge that keeps things real. A little bit rebellious, a little bit nostalgic, it's just right for when you want something short, strong and to the point, but never lacking in depth. Stir thoughtfully while thinking of past loves and adventures yet to come. Crashing an ex's wedding is optional but not recommended.

Ingredients

Serves: 1

50 ml (1¾ oz) mezcal

5 ml (1 tsp) Smoky Syrup (see below) or Simple Syrup (see page 15)

2–3 dashes of orange bitters

ice cubes, for the jug and the glass

1 piece of orange peel, to garnish

For the Smoky Syrup

100 ml (3½ oz) maple syrup

25 ml (¾ oz) water

½ tsp hot smoked paprika

Method

1. For the syrup, place the maple syrup and water in a small saucepan over a medium heat and bring to the boil. Reduce the heat and add the smoked paprika, then simmer for 5 minutes, stirring occasionally. Leave to cool, then pour into a container.

2. Combine the mezcal, syrup and orange bitters in a small jug, add a handful of ice and stir well.

3. Place a large cube of ice or several cubes into a rock or lowball glass. Strain over the drink. Twist the orange peel, skin side down, over the drink, then rub it around the rim of a glass and drop it into the drink.

SOUNDTRACK: 'Friends in Low Places' by Garth Brooks

Strawberry Wine Cooler

This uncomplicated drink is the ideal pairing with Deana Carter's wistful song about the simplicity and freedom of first love, where everything is new and you can only live in the moment. It will remind you of sneaking out to meet your beau on romantic moonlit nights in the height of July and encapsulate all the nostalgia we love to feel when looking back on our past, more innocent selves.

Ingredients

Serves: 1

4 strawberries, about 75 g (3 oz), plus 1 to garnish

1 tsp sugar

ice cubes, for the glass

150 ml (¼ pt) dry white wine

2.5 ml (½ tsp) rose water (optional)

soda or sparkling water, chilled, to top

mint sprigs, to garnish

Method

1. Place the strawberries and sugar into a small jug and, using a hand-held blender, blitz to make a purée. Press the purée through a sieve into a large wine glass, to remove the seeds.

2. Add a large handful of ice to the glass and pour over the wine and rose water, if using. Stir well, then top up with the soda or sparkling water.

3. Garnish with the mint sprigs and a strawberry.

SOUNDTRACK: 'Strawberry Wine' by Deana Carter

Long Islands in the Stream

Some people think Long Island iced tea has its roots in Tennessee during the Prohibition Era, when hard liquor was secretly added to iced tea. This version was created in New York in the seventies – but as Coca-Cola was invented in Atlanta, it still has one foot firmly in the South. This recipe makes for a seriously punchy drink that doesn't hold back, which is just as you would expect from a cocktail to accompany a song written by the Bee Gees and sung by two of country music's biggest legends.

Ingredients

Serves: 1

15 ml (1 tbsp) tequila
15 ml (1 tbsp) vodka
15 ml (1 tbsp) gin
15ml (1 tbsp) white rum
15 ml (1 tbsp) triple sec
15 ml (1 tbsp) freshly squeezed lime juice
ice cubes, for the shaker and the glass
cola, chilled, to top

3 thin lime slices and a stirrer, to garnish

Method

1. Place all the liquid ingredients, apart from the cola, into a cocktail shaker along with some ice cubes, then stir with a spoon until well mixed and the shaker is cold.

2. Add a little more ice to a chilled tall glass, strain over the contents from the shaker and top up with the cola.

3. Garnish with the lime slices and serve with a stirrer.

SOUNDTRACK: 'Islands in the Stream' by Dolly Parton and Kenny Rogers

Achy Breaky Bloody Mary

There's no such thing as a guilty pleasure, whether that's this weekend brunch-time classic or Billy Ray Cyrus' cheesy nineties hit. So grab the tomato juice and the vodka and line dance around the kitchen to country music's beloved slightly embarrassing dad as you whip up the perfect bloody Mary.

Ingredients

Serves: 1

50 ml (1¾ oz) vodka
200 ml (8 oz) tomato juice, chilled
15 ml (1 tbsp) freshly squeezed lemon juice
6 dashes of Worcestershire sauce
4–6 dashes of hot pepper sauce, to taste
pinch of black pepper
ice cubes, for the shaker

1 celery stick, for stirring
1 lemon wedge, to garnish

For the salt rim
1 small lemon wedge
½ tsp celery salt

Method

1. First, prepare the glass. Rub the lemon wedge around the edge of a highball glass, place the celery salt on a small plate and dip in the rim of the glass to coat. Stand the glass upright and leave to dry.

2. Add all the liquid ingredients and a little black pepper to a cocktail shaker with a large handful of ice. Shake until the shaker is cold to the touch.

3. Strain into the glass, serve with the celery stick for stirring and garnish with a lemon wedge.

SOUNDTRACK: 'Achy Breaky Heart' by Billy Ray Cyrus

Honky Tonk Hurricane

Big, boozy and bold, this is a Category 5 cocktail that speaks of chance encounters with old flames as you lock eyes across a neon-lit bar. It's bittersweet and heady, just like those powerful feelings that just won't go away. The combination of two different rums with citrus and passion fruit flavours makes for an unforgettable combination. Based on a New Orleans classic, it's perfect for a stormy night when anything could happen.

Ingredients

Serves: 1

25 ml (¾ oz) white rum

25 ml (¾ oz) dark rum

freshly squeezed juice of ½ orange

freshly squeezed juice of 1 lime

10 ml (2 tsp) Simple Syrup (see page 15)

5 ml (1 tsp) grenadine

1 passion fruit, pulp and seeds

ice cubes, for the shaker and the glass

2 cocktail cherries and 1 orange wheel, to garnish

Method

1. Place all the liquid ingredients, the passion fruit pulp and seeds and a handful of ice into a cocktail shaker. Shake for about 20 seconds or until the shaker is really cold.

2. Fill a hurricane glass with ice and strain the cocktail over the ice.

3. Skewer the cherries and orange wheel onto a cocktail stick and use to garnish the glass.

SOUNDTRACK: 'Hurricane' by Luke Combs

Wildflowers and Whiskey

Get out onto the wide-open plains with this deliciously earthy but floral treat that will make you feel like you are horseback riding down a dirt track with the wind in your hair. The lavender liqueur and honey bring a hint of prairie meadow that's offset by the sharpness of the lemon. And the slug of whiskey is what every cowgirl or outlaw wants at the end of a long day.

Ingredients

Serves: 1

5 ml (1 tsp) honey

5 ml (1 tsp) just-boiled water

50 ml (1¾ oz) floral whiskey

20 ml (4 tsp) lavender liqueur

15 ml (1 tbsp) freshly squeezed lemon juice

ice cubes, for the glass

soda water, chilled, to top

edible wildflowers, to garnish

Method

1. Place the honey into a small heatproof bowl, add the hot water and stir until mixed.

2. Add to a highball glass, then add the whiskey, lavender liqueur and lemon juice, stir well, then add some ice.

3. Top up with soda water, stir again and garnish with wildflowers.

SOUNDTRACK: 'Wildflowers and Wild Horses' by Lainey Wilson

9 to 5 O'Clock
Somewhere

Whether you're relaxing by a pool mid-afternoon or you've just clocked off for the day, this delicious drink is sure to make you come alive. So grab your blender, give the ice a little shake so it sounds like the typewriter noise at the start of the song, and whip up this over-the-top classic. With its cherry and pineapple garnish, this drink is to cocktails what shoulder pads and perms were to the eighties. Bad bosses beware.

Ingredients

Serves: 1

- 60 ml (2 oz) white rum
- 75 ml (2¾ oz) pineapple juice
- 60 ml (2 oz) coconut cream
- 10 ml (2 tsp) Simple Syrup (see page 15)
- ice cubes, for the blender and the glass

- 1 pineapple wedge and/or cherry, to garnish

Method

1. Place all the liquid ingredients into a blender with a small handful of ice. Blitz until smooth, then pour into a piña colada glass with a little ice.

2. Garnish with a wedge of pineapple and/or a cherry skewered on a cocktail stick, if using.

SOUNDTRACK: '9 to 5' by Dolly Parton

Ring of Fireball

This song is such a familiar classic that it's easy to overlook the story behind it. June Carter wrote this song for 'the man in black' when he was still married to his first wife. Falling in love with the wrong person is certainly a dicey situation to be in, but this cocktail brings some irreverence and wit. After all, it's way better to burn your tongue with hot sauce than break your heart on a love that's destined to cause you pain.

Ingredients

Serves: 1

25 ml (¾ oz) cinnamon whiskey
25 ml (¾ oz) white rum
2 drops of hot pepper sauce
ice cubes, for the shaker

Method

1. Place all the ingredients into a cocktail shaker and shake until the shaker is cold.

2. Strain into a shot glass and down in one.

SOUNDTRACK: 'Ring of Fire' by Johnny Cash

Drinkin' 'Bout Me

This fruity, summery drink comes with a real lingering kick from the rum and the lime juice. It may look like an easy-breezy cocktail, but it packs a punch and is certain to reel you in. You might move on to other cocktails, but there will always be the delicious memory of this citrussy, passion-fruit mix ready to tempt you back. Some old flames are hard to put out, after all.

Ingredients

Serves: 1

- 25 ml (¾ oz) white rum
- 25 ml (¾ oz) dark rum
- 25 ml (¾ oz) orange curaçao
- 15 ml (1 tbsp) passion fruit liqueur
- 30 ml (2 tbsp) freshly squeezed lime juice
- 30 ml (2 tbsp) freshly squeezed orange juice
- 5 ml (1 tsp) grenadine
- dash of orange bitters
- ice cubes, for the shaker, plus crushed ice for the glass
- 1 cocktail cherry and a sprig of mint, to garnish

Method

1. Place all the liquid ingredients into a cocktail shaker along with some ice and shake until the shaker is cold.

2. Fill a highball or Collins glass with crushed ice and strain over the cocktail.

3. Garnish with a cocktail cherry and a sprig of mint.

SOUNDTRACK: 'Thinkin' 'Bout Me' by Morgan Wallen

Something in the Watermelon Daiquiri

Nothing says long Southern summer nights like a daiquiri. This is a cool, restorative drink that will revive you and put joy in your heart on even the sultriest evening. Wherever you are in the world, you'll be able to hear the crickets chirping and the distant sound of a lonely goods train rolling along the tracks when you whip up this gorgeous treat for your buddies.

Ingredients

Serves: 1

150 g (5 oz) seedless watermelon chunks
50 ml (2 oz) white rum
30 ml (2 tbsp) freshly squeezed lime juice
5 ml (1 tsp) agave syrup
ice cubes, for the shaker

1 wedge of watermelon, to garnish

For the salt rim
2 tsp sea salt
1 small lime wedge

Method

1. Place the watermelon chunks in a blender and blitz until smooth. Pour through a fine sieve into a small bowl, pressing the fruit with the back of a spoon. Discard the solids and chill the juice.

2. For the salt rim, put the salt on a plate. Rub the rim of a coupe glass with the lime and dip into the salt. Stand the glass upright and let to dry.

3. Place the watermelon juice, rum, lime juice and agave syrup into a cocktail shaker with a handful of ice and shake until the shaker is cold.

4. Strain into the prepared glass and serve immediately with a wedge of watermelon.

SOUNDTRACK: 'Something in the Water' by Carrie Underwood

Spicy Margaritaville

This is a classic margarita but with a sting in its tail. If, like Jimmy Buffett in his song about aimlessly passing time, you need a kick up the ass, this is a cocktail to wake you up and let you know you're alive. Just be careful about what kind of chillies you choose; making the wrong call won't be quite as bad as waking up with a terrible tattoo that you don't remember getting, but there will still be consequences!

Ingredients

Serves: 1

50 ml (1¾ oz) tequila
30 ml (2 tbsp) freshly squeezed lime juice
25 ml (¾ oz) Chilli Syrup (see below)
ice cubes, for the shaker

red chilli slices and a lime wheel, to garnish

For the Chilli Syrup
1 red chilli, sliced
50 g (1¾ oz) caster (baker's) sugar
50 ml (1¾ oz) water

For the rim
½ tsp hot chilli powder
1 tsp lime zest
1 tsp sea salt
1 lime wedge

Method

1. To make the syrup, place all the ingredients into a saucepan and simmer over a low heat, stirring until the sugar has dissolved. Remove from the heat and leave to cool.

2. Next prepare the glass. Place the chilli powder, lime zest and salt on a small plate and mix together, then run the lime wedge along the rim of a martini glass and dip the rim into the salt mix. Stand the glass upright and leave to dry.

3. Place the tequila, lime juice, chilli syrup and a large handful of ice into a cocktail shaker. Shake well until the shaker is really cold.

4. Strain into the glass and garnish with the chilli slices and a lime wheel.

SOUNDTRACK: 'Margaritaville' by Jimmy Buffett

I'm Not Americano's Sweetheart

Not everyone loves Campari; it's bitter, a little spicy and not much of a crowd-pleaser. But you know what? Who cares? Those who think it's too much can go drink something else. This cocktail is for those who dance to the beat of their own drum, who say it as they see it and reckon other people should stick to their own damn business.

Ingredients

Serves: 1

45 ml (1½ oz) Campari
45 ml (1½ oz) sweet vermouth
ice cubes, for the glass
soda water, chilled, to top

1 orange wedge, to garnish

Method

1. Pour the Campari and sweet vermouth into a highball glass filled with ice.

2. Top up with the soda water and stir, then garnish with the orange wedge.

SOUNDTRACK: 'America's Sweetheart' by Elle King

If It Weren't for **the Wine**

Made with still wine, so you can't really call it a spritz, this is an unconventional drink that won't be pigeonholed or tied down. It speaks to a restless spirit, a soul that needs to be on the move, a mind that wants to know what's around the next bend. Sure, that farmhouse idea sure sounds nice, but just like in the song, you can't change your nature to want what you don't want.

Ingredients

Serves: 1

75 ml (3 oz) dry white wine, chilled

45 ml (1½ oz) Campari

ice cubes, for the glass

45 ml (1½ oz) soda water, chilled

2 orange wheels, to garnish

Method

1. Pour the wine and Campari into a wine glass, then half-fill it with ice.

2. Add the soda water and orange wheels and stir gently to mix.

SOUNDTRACK: 'weren't for the wind' by Ella Langley

Tennessee Whiskey Sour

Inspired by a classic country love song that's strangely full of longing, even though the singer seems to be with the person he's in love with, this cocktail is the perfect accompaniment to love stories of all kinds. While the deep caramel of the bourbon suggests sitting on a bar stool until closing time, the lightness of the other ingredients and the irreverence of the cherry garnish make us think of romance and happy endings.

Ingredients

Serves: 1

60 ml (2 oz) bourbon

30 ml (2 tbsp) freshly squeezed lemon juice

15 ml (1 tbsp) Simple Syrup (see page 15)

15 ml (1 tbsp) egg white or aquafaba (chickpea water)

2 drops of Angostura bitters

ice cubes, for the shaker and the glass

1 piece of lemon peel

1 maraschino cherry and 1 orange wheel, to garnish

Method

1. Place all the liquid ingredients into a cocktail shaker and shake for 10 seconds, to combine.

2. Add some ice and shake hard until the cocktail shaker and the ingredients are cold.

3. Place a few ice cubes into a lowball glass. Strain the cocktail over the ice, it should have a thin layer of white froth. Squeeze the lemon peel, skin side down, over the drink to release its oil, then discard the piece of peel.

4. Garnish with a cherry and an orange wheel.

SOUNDTRACK: 'Tennessee Whiskey' by Chris Stapleton

Blue Curaçao
Ain't Your Color

The protagonist in Keith Urban's song sees a woman sitting alone at a bar and decides her man can't be treating her right. Which is kind of presumptuous. Maybe she's had a difficult day at her high-powered job and just wants some peace and quiet? And even if it is man trouble, will another guy hitting on her in the bar really help?! So whip up this cocktail and say, 'Well, actually, blue does suit me, thank you very much!'

Ingredients

Serves: 1

30 ml (2 tbsp) vodka

30 ml (2 tbsp) blue curaçao

30 ml (2 tbsp) freshly squeezed lime juice

ice cubes, for the glass

150 ml (¼ pt) lemonade, chilled, to top

1 maraschino cherry and 1 lemon wheel, to garnish

Method

1. Pour the vodka, blue curaçao and lime juice into a hurricane or highball glass, add the ice and stir until well chilled.

2. Top up with the lemonade and gently stir to combine.

3. Thread the cherry and lemon wheel onto a cocktail stick and use to garnish the glass.

SOUNDTRACK: 'Blue Ain't Your Color' by Keith Urban

Wagon Wheel Wrecker

No wedding in the Southern states would be complete without all the guests swaying and singing along to the Americana classic that is 'Wagon Wheel' – the Old Crow Medicine Show's version or the Darius Rucker one, depending on the vintage of the party attendees. This cocktail is guaranteed to be just as much of a crowd-pleaser – although it is punchy, so be careful things don't get too out of hand. No one wants to be that wedding guest . . . !

Ingredients

Serves: 1

45 ml (1¾ oz) cognac

45 ml (1¾ oz) Southern Comfort

15 ml (1 tbsp) freshly squeezed lemon juice

10 ml (2 tsp) grenadine

ice cubes, for the shaker, plus crushed ice, for the glass

1 lemon wheel, to garnish

Method

1. Pour the cognac, Southern Comfort, lemon juice and grenadine into a cocktail shaker with a handful of ice and shake well, until the shaker is cold.

2. Add some crushed ice to a lowball glass and strain over the cocktail.

3. Add the lemon wheel to garnish.

SOUNDTRACK: 'Wagon Wheel' by Darius Rucker

Fancy
Like Fizz

Whether you're celebrating something special or just excited to have your gang together on a Friday night, this is the perfect drink to make darn sure it feels like an occasion. Peaches bring the Southern charm, while the pink sugar rim says it's party time. So pop the cork and get those boots stomping all over the dancefloor in true cowgirl style.

Ingredients

Serves: 1

1 peach, peeled and roughly chopped

100 ml (3½ oz) prosecco or champagne, chilled, plus extra to top

1 peach slice, to garnish

For the pink sugar rim

15 ml (1 tbsp) granulated sugar

1–2 drops of red or pink gel food dye

1 lemon wedge

Method

1. Place the sugar in a food bag and add a few drops of the gel coloring. Shake well, until you have a pink-colored sugar. Tip out onto a small plate. Rub the rim of a champagne flute with the lemon wedge, then dip the glass into the sugar. Stand the glass upright and allow to dry slightly.

2. Put the peach chunks into a mini food processor and blitz until smooth. Press through a sieve and collect the purée in a small jug, then set in the fridge to chill.

3. Place the peach purée in the bottom of a champagne flute, top with prosecco or champagne and stir well until combined. Top with a little more of the bubbles and serve with a slice of peach.

SOUNDTRACK: 'Fancy Like' by Walker Hayes

Highball Horse

Just like Kacey Musgraves' pop-infused country banger, this straight-up, no-nonsense cocktail is the perfect drink to get the party started. It's cool without being try-hard, making the most of a few great ingredients without attempting to show off with a load of bells and whistles. The pretentious crowd is welcome to saddle up and ride out of town – this drink is classic in exactly the right way.

Ingredients

Serves: 1

45 ml (1¾ oz) brandy

ice cubes, for the glass

125 ml (4 oz) ginger beer, chilled, to top

1 long piece of lemon peel, to garnish

Method

1. Pour the brandy into a highball glass and add the ice.

2. Top up with the ginger beer, stir gently, then garnish with the lemon twist.

SOUNDTRACK: 'High Horse' by Kacey Musgraves

Son of a Sinnerman

This is a sweet and earthy take on a cool noughties cocktail that speaks to coming in off the highway and sitting in a who-knows-where bar late into the evening, with nothing in mind but the next destination. It's the freedom of the open road mixed with a tinge of regret and restlessness that just won't be sated. In fact, it's an age-old Deep South story in a glass.

Ingredients

Serves: 1

50 ml (1¾ oz) coffee-spiced rum
10 ml (2 tsp) maple syrup
10 ml (2 tsp) vermouth rosso
2 dashes of chocolate bitters
2 large ice cubes, for the glass

1 piece of orange peel, to garnish

Method

1. Pour the rum, maple syrup and vermouth into a cocktail shaker, add the chocolate bitters, then stir well.

2. Place 2 large ice cubes in an old fashioned or shortball glass and pour over the cocktail.

3. Garnish with a twist of orange.

SOUNDTRACK: 'Son of a Sinner' by Jelly Roll

Take Me Home, Cosmo Roads

The pink of sunset over those famous West Virginian mountains, this cocktail is – like the song it's named after – a nailed-on classic. When you want to get back to something comfortingly familiar, this is guaranteed to deliver. So grab your shaker, find some old-timey bluegrass music and hum along, as you dream of driving along dirt roads past blue-tinged mountains with winding rivers in misty valleys below. *Actually* heaven.

Ingredients

Serves: 1

50 ml (2 oz) lemon vodka or vodka

90 ml (3 oz) cranberry juice, chilled

30 ml (2 tbsp) Cointreau or triple sec

30 ml (2 tbsp) freshly squeezed lime juice

ice cubes, for the shaker

1 piece of orange and/or lime peel, to garnish

Method

1. Place all the ingredients, except for the garnish, in a cocktail shaker with a handful of ice. Shake until the shaker is cold.

2. Strain into a chilled martini glass and serve garnished with the orange and/or lime twist.

SOUNDTRACK: 'Take Me Home, Country Roads' by John Denver

Texas
Hold My Cocktail

Cards on the table – this sweet whiskey drink might not be what you'd associate with dancefloor queen Beyoncé, but in the song she tells us to pour sugar on honey, and who are we not to do what Queen Bey says? Even if there is no tornado warning currently in your city, you can still hunker down with a glass of this straight-up lemon and whiskey concoction and not even care what the elements are serving up outdoors.

Ingredients

Serves: 1

- 15 ml (1 tbsp) honey
- 15 ml (1 tbsp) boiling water
- 60 ml (2 oz) bourbon or other whiskey
- 30 ml (2 tbsp) freshly squeezed lemon juice
- ice cubes, for the shaker

- 1 piece of lemon peel, to garnish

Method

1. Pour the honey and boiling water into the bottom of a cocktail shaker and stir until the honey has dissolved. Allow to cool.

2. Add the bourbon and lemon juice with a large handful of ice and shake well, until the shaker is cold.

3. Strain into a coupe glass and serve with a twist of lemon.

SOUNDTRACK: 'TEXAS HOLD 'EM' by Beyoncé

When It Rains It Pours Whiskey

This song celebrates a run of great 'redneck' luck that starts when the protagonist breaks up with his girlfriend. We all know what it's like to get out of a doomed, negative relationship, to feel the clouds part and for everything to come good again. Well, you can make your own luck by mixing up this delicious, boozy drink that's perfect to celebrate the great things that are certain to come your way soon.

Ingredients

Serves: 1

ice cubes, for the glass
30 ml (2 tbsp) whiskey
30 ml (2 tbsp) Irish cream liqueur
15 ml (1 tbsp) coffee liqueur

Method

1. Place the ice in a small tumbler, then pour over the whiskey, Irish cream and coffee liqueurs. Stir well and serve.

SOUNDTRACK: 'When It Rains It Pours' by Luke Combs

Need
Brew Now

Whether it's a quarter past one and you need to keep the party going, or you're just getting warmed up, an espresso martini is what we all need right now. The key is freshly made coffee that's been allowed to cool – don't go melting that ice, y'all! Shake it like you mean it, strain and feel the buzz. Then get back on the dancefloor and forget about that no-good ex!

Ingredients

Serves: 1

50 ml (2 oz) vodka

25 ml (¾ oz) coffee liqueur

1 shot of espresso, cooled (about 25 ml/¾ oz)

5 ml (1 tsp) Simple Syrup (see page 15)

ice cubes, for the shaker

3 coffee beans, to garnish

Method

1. Place all the liquid ingredients into a cocktail shaker along with the ice. Shake really vigorously for 30 seconds, as this will create the creamy top.

2. Strain into a chilled martini glass and garnish with the coffee beans.

SOUNDTRACK: 'Need You Now' by Lady A

Gin McGraw

While there are loads of break-your-heart country songs that are about looking back with regret, Taylor's first single is more about celebrating something that was lovely while it lasted, rather than crying over what might have been. The rose petals in this cocktail add an extra sprinkling of romance, and the lychee juice brings a certain sophistication – just like the wise-beyond-her-years sound of Taylor herself.

Ingredients

Serves: 1

60 ml (2 oz) gin

30 ml (2 tbsp) freshly squeezed lime juice

60 ml (2 oz) lychee juice, chilled

5–10 ml (1–2 tsp) rose syrup, to taste

ice cubes, for the shaker

dried rose petals and a lime wedge, to garnish

Method

1. Place all the liquid ingredients into a cocktail shaker along with some ice, then shake until the shaker is really cold.

2. Strain into a martini glass and serve garnished with some rose petals and a lime wedge.

SOUNDTRACK: 'Tim McGraw' by Taylor Swift

(I Never Promised You a) Rosé Garden

Lynn Anderson might be giving us the very wise advice that real love is never going to be fairytale perfection - life is more complicated than that - but this cocktail comes close. A little sweet but not sugary, it's the perfect drink for making the most of a gorgeous summer afternoon and appreciating the good times. While you can't avoid the rainy days, you can always rely on the sun to come back out again.

Ingredients

Serves: 1

25 ml (4 oz) dry rosé wine, chilled
30 ml (2 tbsp) raspberry liqueur
15 ml (1 tbsp) orange liqueur
large handful of ice, for the glass
4 raspberries
2–3 strawberries, sliced
2 thin orange slices

sprigs of mint, to garnish
lime soda water, chilled, to top

Method

1. Pour the wine, raspberry and orange liqueurs into a large wine glass and stir well.

2. Add the ice, stir gently, then add the fruit and mint sprigs. Top up with the soda water and stir gently to mix.

SOUNDTRACK: '(I Never Promised You a) Rose Garden' by Lynn Anderson

Mai Tai
Church

Nothing says summer like a playful and thirst-quenching mai tai. It's fun, fruity and just a little bit extra. Whether you're at a roadside juke joint at the end of a day rolling along the great American highway, or just sitting in the kitchen following a sweaty commute home from work, it's certain to revive your soul and it's definitely good enough to worship. Let me hear you say Amen!

Ingredients

Serves: 1

30 ml (2 tbsp) white rum

30 ml (2 tbsp) dark rum

30 ml (2 tbsp) orange curaçao or triple sec

15 ml (1 tbsp) almond syrup

30 ml (2 tbsp) freshly squeezed lime juice

30 ml (2 tbsp) freshly squeezed orange juice

30 ml (2 tbsp) fresh pineapple juice, chilled

ice cubes, for the shaker and the glass

1 pineapple wedge and a maraschino cherry, to garnish

Method

1. Add all the liquid ingredients to a cocktail shaker with a large handful of ice. Shake well until combined and the shaker is very cold.

2. Strain into an ice-filled lowball glass.

3. Skewer the pineapple wedge and cherry onto a cocktail stick and balance on the glass.

SOUNDTRACK: 'My Church' by Maren Morris

Hazy

Celebrate this absolute country classic of longing famously written by Willie Nelson with a drink that's as deep and dark as the night gathering outside the bar windows. It's sweet and long, just right to accompany a song that, while short in lyrics, lingers in the heart and the mind, capturing the very essence of a love that was never destined to last.

Ingredients

Serves: 1

45 ml (1½ oz) vodka

15 ml (1 tbsp) black raspberry liqueur

15 ml (1 tbsp) blue curaçao

15 ml (1 tbsp) freshly squeezed lime juice

ice cubes, for the shaker and the glass

50 ml (1¾ oz) cranberry juice, chilled

sprigs of mint and 1–2 blackberries, to garnish

Method

1. Place the vodka, liqueurs and lime juice into a cocktail shaker with the ice. Shake well until the shaker is cold.

2. Add some ice to a short glass, strain over the contents of the shaker, then add the cranberry juice and stir well.

3. Drop the mint sprigs into the glass, then thread the blackberries onto a cocktail stick and use to garnish, too.

SOUNDTRACK: 'Crazy' by Patsy Cline

Paloma
Smokeshow

This drink takes the sophisticated paloma and gives it some small-town authenticity and bite. Pink-tinged, sweet, sour and smoky, it's like a once-elegant dress that's started to get a raggedy hem being worn with no-nonsense boots. So shake one up as you think about bad-news boys in pick-up trucks. Just remember to enjoy the drama but leave the poor decisions to the woman in Zach Bryan's song.

Ingredients

Serves: 1

50 ml (1¾ oz) mezcal or tequila blanco

50 ml (1¾ oz) freshly squeezed pink grapefruit juice

10 ml (2 tsp) freshly squeezed lime juice

10 ml (2 tsp) Smoky Syrup (see page 53)

ice cubes, for the shaker and the glass

soda water, chilled, to top

grapefruit wedge and/or lime wheel, to garnish

For the salt rim

1 tsp sea salt

1 lime wedge

Method

1. First, prepare the glass. Place the salt on a small plate, run the lime wedge along the rim of a highball glass, then dip the glass into the salt. Stand the glass upright and leave to dry.

2. Pour all the liquid ingredients, except the soda water, into a cocktail shaker along with a handful of ice. Shake until the shaker is really cold.

3. Strain into a glass, add a couple of ice cubes and top up with the soda water.

4. Garnish with the grapefruit wedge and/or lime wheel.

SOUNDTRACK: 'Oklahoma Smokeshow' by Zach Bryan

Limoncello
Like You Mean It

Limoncello might seem like something you'd associate more with the hillside villages of southern Italy, but country music has always incorporated a surprising number of influences, so there's no reason why country-music-inspired cocktails shouldn't, too. This zingy drink perfectly combines Latin passion with straight-talking Southern attitude. With all that citrus, it's upfront and not shy to get fresh.

Ingredients

Serves: 1

- 2 sprigs of lemon thyme, plus extra to garnish
- 50 ml (2 oz) gin
- 45 ml (3 tbsp) limoncello
- 30 ml (2 tbsp) freshly squeezed lime juice
- ice cubes, for the shaker, plus 1 large ice cube for the glass
- soda water, chilled, to top
- 1 piece of lemon peel, to garnish

Method

1. Place the thyme sprigs into the bottom of a cocktail shaker and muddle, to release the flavour. Pour in the gin, limoncello and lime juice and add a large handful of ice cubes. Shake for 20 seconds or until the shaker is very cold.

2. Add some ice cubes to a lowball glass and strain over the cocktail.

3. Garnish the glass with a twist of lemon and add some thyme sprigs.

SOUNDTRACK: 'Love Me Like You Mean It' by Kelsea Ballerini

Goodbye
Earl Grey Sour

This is a classy cocktail that feels a bit special – perfect to make for that ride-or-die friend who you know will always have your back, no matter what happens. Hopefully you'll never be in a position like Wanda and Mary Anne in the song, faced with an abusive man and only one solution . . . But as none of us can know what's coming down the road, we need to keep our besties close and make sure they know how much we appreciate them.

Ingredients

Serves: 1

50 ml (1¾ oz) Earl Grey gin (see below)

15 ml (1 tbsp) Simple Syrup (see page 15)

30 ml (2 tbsp) freshly squeezed lemon juice

ice cubes, for the shaker

1 egg white or aquafaba (chickpea water)

1 lemon wheel, to garnish

For the Earl Grey gin

200 ml (7 oz) dry gin

45 g (3 tbsp) Earl Grey tea leaves

Method

1. To make the Earl Grey gin, pour the gin into a jug, add the tea leaves, cover and leave to infuse for 1 hour, then strain into a jug. Store any leftover Earl Grey gin in an airtight container in the fridge, it will keep for up to 1 month.

2. Pour 50 ml (1¾ oz) of the Earl Grey gin, plus the syrup and the lemon juice into a cocktail shaker along with some ice, then shake until the shaker is really cold.

3. Strain the mixture into a jug and discard the ice. Return the liquid to the shaker with the egg white and shake vigorously for 10 seconds, then strain into a coupe glass and garnish with a lemon wheel.

SOUNDTRACK: 'Goodbye Earl' by The Chicks

Sweet Vermouth
Alabama

This cocktail is just as much of a crowd-pleaser as Lynyrd Skynyrd's classic about the Southern state. You don't need to have beef with Neil Young to whip up this sweet and smoky drink. So gather your kin – whatever that means to you – stick on the song and, well, *turn it up!* A good singalong can cure so many of the things that ail us.

Ingredients

Serves: 1

25 ml (¾ oz) sweet vermouth

50 ml (1¾ oz) bourbon

5 ml (1 tsp) syrup from a jar of maraschino cherries

dash of bitters

ice cubes, for the jug

1 maraschino cherry and a piece of lemon peel, to garnish

Method

1. Pour all the liquid ingredients into a small jug with the ice and stir well.

2. Strain into a martini glass and garnish with the cherry and a twist of lemon.

SOUNDTRACK: 'Sweet Home Alabama' by Lynyrd Skynyrd

Drinkin' After Midnight

Maybe the walk home from the bar is with a beau, maybe it's with a friend as you discuss and dissect the gossip from the evening. This is the perfect nightcap if you want to cosy up on the sofa when you get in, especially when the weather is getting colder and the nights are drawing in. It's a little dessert-in-a-glass that will warm you right through.

Ingredients

Serves: 1

5 ml (1 tsp) maple syrup

2.5 ml (½ tsp) vanilla extract

pinch of ground cinnamon

pinch of ground nutmeg, plus extra to garnish

pinch of ground allspice

60 ml (2 oz) dark rum

100 ml (3½ oz) boiling water, or as needed

1 tsp softened butter

Method

1. Place the maple syrup, vanilla and spices in a mug or latte glass and stir to mix well.

2. Add the rum, then pour over the hot water, top with the softened butter and stir to mix and melt the butter.

3. Sprinkle with the ground nutmeg to serve.

SOUNDTRACK: 'Walkin' After Midnight' by Patsy Cline

Sloe Burn

This is the perfect drink for a golden late-summer evening, when it feels like everything is slowing down ready for autumn. It'll take a few minutes to make the ginger syrup, but don't worry about that - just like Kacey Musgraves tells us, it's good when we take our time and stop to appreciate what's going on around us. Just imagine you're looking out over the Cumberland River and enjoy a moment to chill.

Ingredients

Serves: 1

60 ml (2 oz) sloe gin
25 ml (1 oz) freshly squeezed lemon juice
10 ml (2 tsp) Ginger Syrup (see below)
ice cubes, for the shaker
soda water, chilled, to top

1 lemon wheel and 1 blackberry, to garnish

For the Ginger Syrup

150 g (5 oz) caster (baker's) sugar
100 ml (3¾ oz) water
125 g (4 oz) piece of fresh root ginger, peeled and chopped

Method

1. First make the ginger syrup. Place the sugar, water and ginger in a small pan over a gentle heat and cook, stirring, for 2–3 minutes, until the sugar has dissolved. Simmer for 20 minutes. Allow to cool in the pan to allow the flavours to develop, then strain the syrup into a container. It will keep in the fridge for up to 3 weeks.

2. Add the sloe gin, lemon juice and ginger syrup to a cocktail shaker with a large handful of ice, then shake until the shaker is very cold.

3. Strain into a highball glass and top up with the soda water. Garnish with a lemon wheel and a blackberry.

SOUNDTRACK: 'Slow Burn' by Kacey Musgraves

French 23

The original French 75 was named after a type of gun, which is kind of fitting for a cocktail inspired by Chayce Beckham's song, whose protagonist has travelled all over the US and is wearied by his experiences, feeling like a 'stagecoach shotgun'. But if we have learned anything, it's that when life gives us lemon liqueur, we should damn well put some champagne in it! So make this for your ride-or-dies and swap stories from the road.

Ingredients

Serves: 1

60 ml (2 oz) gin
30 ml (2 tbsp) lemon liqueur
ice cubes, for the shaker
champagne, chilled, to top

1 piece of lemon peel, to garnish

Method

1. Add the gin, lemon liqueur and a handful of ice to a cocktail shaker. Shake for 30 seconds until the shaker is cold.

2. Strain into a champagne flute and top up with the champagne.

3. Garnish with a twist of lemon.

SOUNDTRACK: '23' by Chayce Beckham

Buy
Dirty Martini

This salty drink keeps it real. Like the wisdom handed down in the song, it's clear, honest and tells it how it is. Sure, sometimes you want a fun cocktail with all the razzamatazz, but this is for the times when you need something upfront and simple after a long day at work. Whether you were out mending fences on the ranch or had way too many Zoom calls, this drink delivers.

Ingredients

Serves: 1

50 ml (2 oz) gin or vodka
10 ml (2 tsp) dry vermouth
15 ml (1 tbsp) olive brine
ice cubes, for the shaker

3 pitted green olives, to garnish

Method

1. Place the gin or vodka, vermouth and olive brine in a cocktail shaker, add a large handful of ice and shake until the shaker is really cold.

2. Strain into a martini glass, thread the olives onto a cocktail stick and use to garnish.

SOUNDTRACK: 'Buy Dirt' by Jordan Davis and Luke Bryan

Mean Mojito

When you need something sparkly and refreshing to pick you up and help you brush off someone's negative energy, this classic mojito is sure to hit the spot. It's a little bit sweet and a little bit sour – just right for reminding yourself that you're too classy to let anyone's mean spirit drag you down. Leave those bad vibes in the rearview mirror and get your real friends together to celebrate the power of cheering each other on.

Ingredients

Serves: 1

- 2 limes, each cut into 8 wedges
- 1 tsp granulated sugar
- 6 fresh mint leaves
- 60 ml (2 oz) white rum
- ice cubes, for the glass
- 100 ml (3½ oz) soda or sparkling water, chilled
- 1 sprig of mint, to garnish

Method

1. Place the lime quarters (reserving 2 to garnish), sugar and mint leaves in a jug and muddle together until the lime juice has been released and the mint is torn up.

2. Pour the rum into the bottom of a tall glass. Strain the lime mixture over the rum and add some ice cubes. Pour over the soda or sparkling water to taste.

3. Stir and garnish with the reserved lime wedges and a sprig of mint.

SOUNDTRACK: 'Mean' by Taylor Swift

Long Long Tom Collins

Just because you know it's never going to happen, that doesn't mean it's easy to get them out of your head. So Linda tells us in her song for the heartsore and lovesick. Some things stick around a lot longer than you want them to, but others endure for better reasons. This OG drink has been served in bars for 150 years, purely because it's simple and delicious. Maybe just try to overlook the fact it's named after a guy . . .

Ingredients

Serves: 1

ice cubes, for the glass

50 ml (1¾ oz) gin

25 ml (¾ oz) freshly squeezed lemon juice

15 ml (1 tbsp) Simple Syrup (see page 15)

125 ml (4 oz) soda water, chilled, or to top

1 lemon wheel, to garnish

Method

1. Fill a Collins or highball glass with ice, add the gin, lemon juice and syrup and stir well, then top up with the soda water.

2. Garnish with the lemon wheel.

SOUNDTRACK: 'Long Long Time' by Linda Ronstadt

Index

agave syrup 38–9, 70–1
allspice 114–15
almond syrup 102–3
amaretto 32–3
Angostura bitters 20–1, 34–5, 42–3, 78–9
Aperol 6–7
apple liqueur 18–19

black raspberry liqueur 44–5, 104–5
bloody mary
  Achy Breaky Bloody Mary 58–9
blue curaçao 46–7, 80–1, 104–5
blue lagoon
  Blue Curaçao Ain't Your Color 80–1
bourbon
  Red Solo Royale 44–5
  Sweet Vermouth Alabama 112–13
  Tennessee Whiskey Sour 78–9
  Texas Hold My Cocktail 92–3
  Whiskey on My Mind 36–7
brandy 28–9, 86–7

Campari 26–7, 74–5, 76–7
champagne 44–5, 84–5, 118–19
cherry liqueur 34–5

chilli 38–9, 72–3
Chilli Syrup 72–3
chocolate bitters 88–9
cinnamon 114–15
cinnamon whiskey 66–7
coconut cream 64–5
coffee liqueur 94–5, 96–7
cognac 22–3, 82–3
Cointreau 90–1
cranberry juice 16–17, 90–1, 104–5
crème de violette 30–1, 46–7

daiquiri
  Something in the Watermelon Daiquiri 70–1
dry vermouth 120–1

Earl Grey gin 110–11
egg white/aquafaba 32–3, 78–9, 110–11
elderflower liqueur 40–1
espresso 96–7
espresso martini
  Need Brew Now 96–7

gin
  Aust-Gin Aviation 30–1
  Boot Scootin' Spritz 40–1
  Buy Dirty Martini 120–1
  French 23 118–19

Gin McGraw 98–9
I Walk the Lime 10–11
Limoncello Like You Mean It 108–9
Long Islands in the Stream 56–7
Long Long Tom Collins 124–5
Neon Moon Martini 46–7
No Shoes, No Shirt Negroni 26–7
Slim Pickle 18–19
The Giver Gimlet 24–5
see also Earl Grey gin; sloe gin
ginger beer
  6 Mules Later 20–1
  Highball Horse 86–7
  I Will Always Love Yuzu 50–1
  Shaboozey Sling 42–3
Ginger Syrup 36–7, 116–17
glass rims
  chilli 72–3
  salt 12–13, 58–9, 70–1, 106–7
  sugar 48–9, 84–5
grapefruit juice 48–9, 106–7
grenadine 8–9, 60–1, 68–9, 82–3

honey 62–3, 92–3

hot pepper sauce 58–9, 66–7

Irish cream liqueur 94–5

jalapeños 12–13

lager 12–13, 14–15
lavender liqueur 62–3
lemon juice 14–15, 18–19, 22–3, 30–3, 44–9, 58–9, 62–3, 78–9, 82–3, 92–3, 110–11, 124–5
lemon liqueur 118–19
lemon vodka 90–1
lemonade 80–1
Lillet Blanc 28–9
lime juice 8–13, 16–21, 24–5, 38–9, 42–3, 56–7, 60–1, 68–9, 72–3, 80–1, 90–1, 98–9, 102–9
Lime Syrup 24–5
limoncello
  French 23 118–19
  Limoncello Like You Mean It 108–9
lychee juice 98–9

mango juice 8–9
maple syrup 52–3, 88–9, 114–15
maraschino cherry syrup 32–3, 112–13
maraschino liqueur 30–1

margarita
  Cowboy Carter-ita 12–13
  Spicy Margaritaville 72–3
martini
  Buy Dirty Martini 120–1
  Neon Moon Martini 46–7
mezcal 38–9, 52–3, 106–7
mojito 122–3

negroni 26–7

olive brine 120–1
orange bitters 38–9, 52–3, 68–9
orange blossom water 6–7
orange curaçao 68–9, 102–3
orange juice 36–7, 60–1, 68–9, 102–3
orange liqueur 22–3, 100–1
  see also Cointreau; triple sec

paprika 52–3
passion fruit 60–1
passion fruit liqueur 26–7, 68–9
peach 84–5
peach schnapps 16–17, 36–7

pickle juice 18–19
piña colada
  9 to 5 O'Clock Somewhere 64–5
pineapple juice 64–5, 102–3
prosecco
  Boot Scootin' Spritz 40–1
  Fancy Like Fizz 84–5
  Red Solo Royale 44–5
  Something in the Orange Spritz 6–7
purple haze
  Hazy 104–5

raspberry liqueur 100–1
rose flavours 54–5, 98–9
rosé wine 100–1
rum (coffee-spiced) 88–9
rum (dark)
  Drinkin' After Midnight 114–15
  Drinkin' 'Bout Me 68–9
  Honky Tonk Hurricane 60–1
  Mai Tai Church 102–3
rum (white)
  9 to 5 O'Clock Somewhere 64–5
  Drinkin' 'Bout Me 68–9
  Honky Tonk Hurricane 60–1
  Long Islands in the Stream 56–7
  Mai Tai Church 102–3

Mean Mojito 122–3
Ring of Fireball 66–7
Something in the
  Watermelon Daiquiri
  70–1

sake/shochu 50–1
Simple Syrup 14–15,
  60–1, 64–5
sloe gin 116–17
Smoky Syrup 52–3,
  106–7
soda (blood orange) 6–7
soda water 10–11, 40–1,
  54–5, 62–3, 74–7,
  116–17, 122–5
sours
  Follow Your Amaretto
    32–3
  Goodbye Earl Grey
    Sour 110–11
  Tennessee Whiskey
    78–9
Southern Comfort 82–3
sparkling water 54–5,
  122–3
strawberry wine cooler
  54–5
sweet vermouth
  I'm Not Americano's
    Sweetheart 74–5
  Stand by Your
    Manhattan 34–5
  Sweet Vermouth
    Alabama 112–13

tequila
  Cowboy Carter-ita
    12–13
  Jolene's Revenge 38–9
  Long Islands in the
    Stream 56–7
  Long Long Tom Collins
    124–5
  Paloma Smokeshow
    106–7
  Spicy Margaritaville
    72–3
  Tequila Never Broke
    My Heart 8–9
tomato juice 58–9
triple sec
  Cowboy Carter-ita
    12–13
  Long Islands in the
    Stream 56–7
  Mai Tai Church 102–3
  Take Me Home, Cosmo
    Roads 90–1
  Teardrops on My Bar
    Cart 48–9

vermouth rosso 88–9
vodka
  6 Mules Later 20–1
  Achy Breaky Bloody
    Mary 58–9
  Blue Curaçao Ain't
    Your Color 80–1
  Buy Dirty Martini
    120–1

  Hazy 104–5
  Long Islands in the
    Stream 56–7
  Man! I Feel Like a Woo
    Woo 16–17
  Need Brew Now 96–7
  Take Me Home, Cosmo
    Roads 90–1
  Teardrops on My Bar
    Cart 48–9

watermelon 70–1
whiskey
  Save a Horse (Rye'd a
    Cowboy) 14–15
  Shaboozey Sling 42–3
  Stand by Your
    Manhattan 34–5
  Tennessee Whiskey
    Sour 78–9
  Texas Hold My Cocktail
    92–3
  When It Rains It Pours
    Whiskey 94–5
  Whiskey on My Mind
    36–7
  Wildflowers and
    Whiskey 62–3
white wine (dry) 54–5,
  76–7

Yellow Chartreuse 28–9
yuzu juice 50–1